EXTREME SCIENCE EXPLORERS

EXPLORE THE INSIDE OF A TORNADO

Tricia Hoffman

Enslow PUBLISHING

Please visit our website, www.enslow.com. For a free color catalog of all our high-quality books, call toll free 1-800-398-2504 or fax 1-877-980-4454

Published in 2027 by
Enslow Publishing
2544 Clinton Street
Buffalo, NY 14224

Portions of this work were originally authored by Christine Honders and published as *Fantastic Science Journeys: A Trip Inside a Tornado*. All new material in this edition is authored by Tricia Hoffman.

Cataloging-in-Publication Data
ames: Hoffman, Tricia.
Title: Explore the inside of a tornado / Tricia Hoffman.
Description: Buffalo, NY : Enslow Publishing, 2027. | Series: Extreme science explorers | Includes glossary and index.
Identifiers: ISBN 9781978549029 (pbk.) | ISBN 9781978549036 (library bound) | ISBN 9781978549043 (ebook)
Subjects: LCSH: Tornadoes--Juvenile literature.
Classification: LCC QC955.2 H644 2027 | DDC 551.553--dc23

Printed in China

Photos Credits: Cover, p. 1 sdecoret/Shutterstock.com; p. 3 Wira SHK/Shutterstock.com; p. 4 NOAA/NOAA; p. 4 Huntstyle/Shutterstock.com; p. 6 Realstock/Shutterstock.com; p. 8 chris hultner/Shutterstock.com; p. 10 Adansijav Official/Shutterstock.com; p. 10 Joe Belanger/Shutterstock.com; p. 12 logistock/Shutterstock.com; p. 12 Alex Erwin/Shutterstock.com; p. 14 aapsky/Shutterstock.com; p. 15 zombiu26/Shutterstock.com; p. 16 Domenichini Giuliano/Shutterstock.com; p. 19 John D Sirlin/Shutterstock.com; p. 20 Bilanol/Shutterstock.com; p. 22 William A. Morgan/Shutterstock.com; p. 23 Noel V. Baebler/Shutterstock.com; p. 24 Jen Lane Art Photography/Shutterstock.com; p. 24 Dimitrios Karamitros/Shutterstock.com; p. 27 speedshutter Photography/Shutterstock.com; p. 28 Capturing Adventure/Shutterstock.com; p. 31 b113/Shutterstock.com

CPSIA compliance information: Batch #QSENS27: For further information, contact Enslow Publishing, New York, New York, at 1-800-398-2504.

TABLE OF CONTENTS

GET READY FOR A WILD RIDE!

The sky is dark. Rain is pouring. Winds are howling. You've probably seen many thunderstorms. But did you know that a really bad storm can lead to a tornado? You may have seen pictures of tornadoes, but most people have never seen one with their own eyes.

The inside of a tornado is a swirling, **violent** place. What if you could safely see what happens inside? You'd see how a tornado forms and feel how fast it moves. You're in luck! We're about to go on that exact adventure. But buckle up, because it's going to be wild. Let's explore the inside of a tornado!

THAT'S EXTREME!

In 1931, a tornado in Minnesota lifted a railroad train with 117 people on it. It carried the train for 80 feet (24 m)!

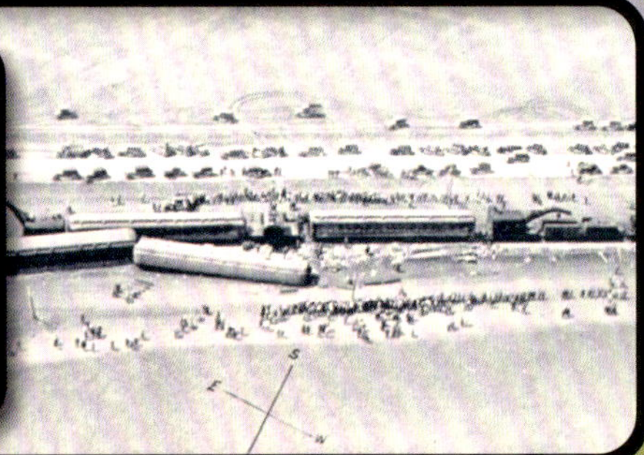

Tornadoes are also known as twisters. Some are weak, but others can be very dangerous.

When extreme weather happens, the safest place to be is inside.

WILD WEATHER

Weather happens all day, every day. It's something we can't control. In fact, it's so powerful that it often controls us! The weather affects what we do, where we live, and even what we wear.

Most of the time, weather is calm. But sometimes the weather turns extreme! Very bad weather is sometimes called extreme weather. **Hurricanes**, snowstorms, and tornadoes don't happen very often. But when they do, they can cause lots of harm to buildings, roads, and even people. Extreme weather can cause extreme damage.

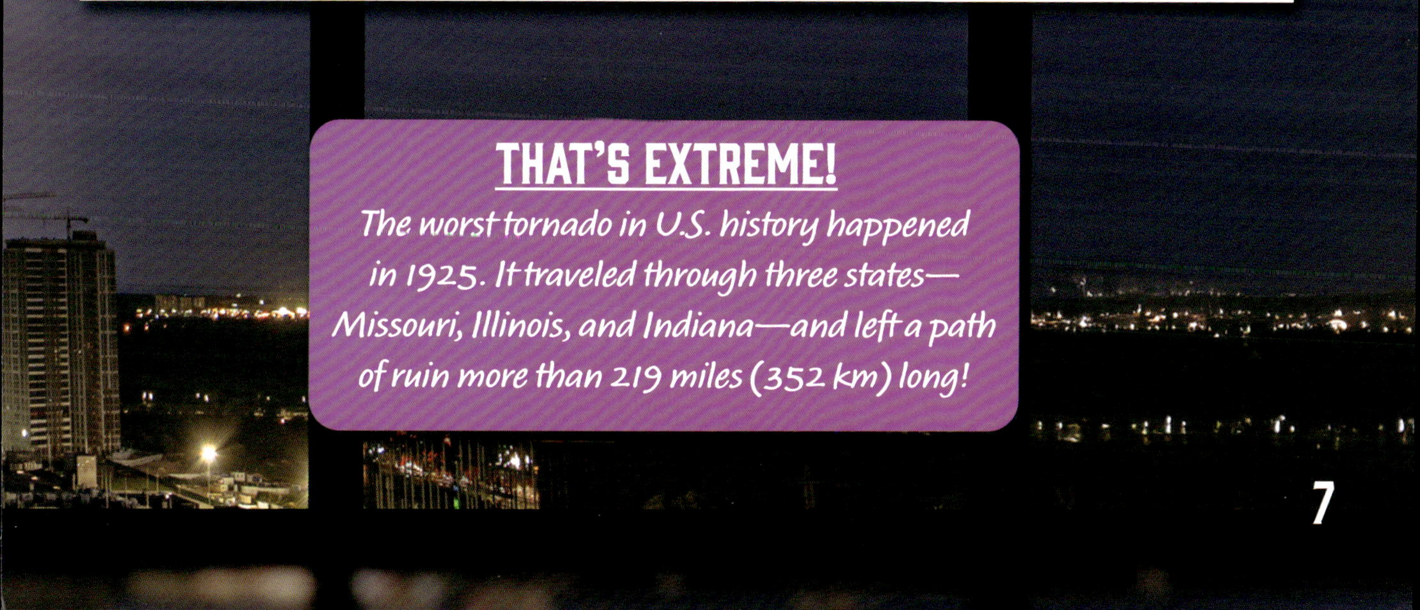

THAT'S EXTREME!

The worst tornado in U.S. history happened in 1925. It traveled through three states—Missouri, Illinois, and Indiana—and left a path of ruin more than 219 miles (352 km) long!

If you are caught outside in a tornado, don't try to outrun it—even if you're in a vehicle! Get to a ditch or other low area and lie flat.

TERRIFYING TORNADOES

Tornadoes are nature's strongest storms. They usually come from powerful thunderstorms. Rotating winds can blow up to 300 miles (483 km) per hour. They are so strong they can pick up cars and toss them through the air! These winds can rip homes apart and even pull the bark off trees.

Tornadoes can also move quickly. Most tornadoes travel about 10 to 20 miles (16 to 32 km) per hour. Other tornadoes are so fast you would have to drive a car more than 70 miles (113 km) per hour to outrun them!

THAT'S EXTREME!

A tornado usually lasts for less than 15 minutes. But in that short time, these storms can cause massive destruction.

TORNADOES IN THE U.S.

The United States has more tornadoes than any other country in the world. About 1,000 tornadoes strike the country every year. Most of them happen in an area that's nicknamed Tornado Alley.

Tornado Alley is the part of the country that stretches from Texas to South Dakota. One reason many tornadoes form here is because the land is very flat. Another reason is that warm, moist air from the South meets with cold, dry air from the North. This combination is perfect for making tornadoes.

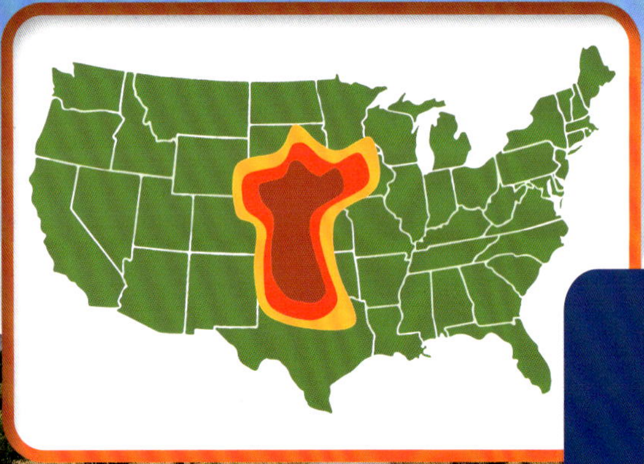

THAT'S EXTREME!

Tornado Alley usually includes South Dakota, Nebraska, Colorado, Kansas, Oklahoma, and Texas, but it may also include Iowa, Wyoming, Minnesota, and other states.

Tornadoes are most common in the spring or early summer. In April 2011, more than 300 tornadoes formed in the U.S. over the course of three days.

CHECKING THE WEATHER

Close to the ground, the air is warm and **humid**. Going higher, the air is colder and drier. This temperature difference is known as **instability**. Instability in the temperature is often a sign that a storm is coming.

THAT'S EXTREME!

*When it's heated, the warm air is less **dense** than the cooler air above it, which causes it to rise.*

Suddenly, a warm breeze blows up from the ground. The wind pushes upward. That's because the sun heated up the air near the ground, making it very light and causing it to rise quickly. This is called an **updraft**. The updraft carries water vapor into the **atmosphere**.

Before tornadoes form, the wind dies down and the air can become very still. You should watch the sky for a greenish color or low, dark clouds.

A TORNADO BEGINS

Water vapor can't be seen, but when it reaches cool air, it forms clouds and turns into rain. The rain starts to fall.

As the rain falls, it pulls air down with it. The rain becomes so heavy that it creates a **downdraft**. The updraft and downdraft get stronger and carry the water vapor around and around in a circle! Updrafts and downdrafts moving quickly create dangerous opportunities for extreme weather such as tornadoes.

THAT'S EXTREME!

Sometimes updrafts carry raindrops so high they freeze. They jump back and forth in the updraft and downdraft, getting bigger until they fall as hail. The largest hailstone ever measured weighed 2 pounds (0.9 kg)!

Tornadoes can form very quickly in ***unstable*** weather. Tornadoes and hail often occur together.

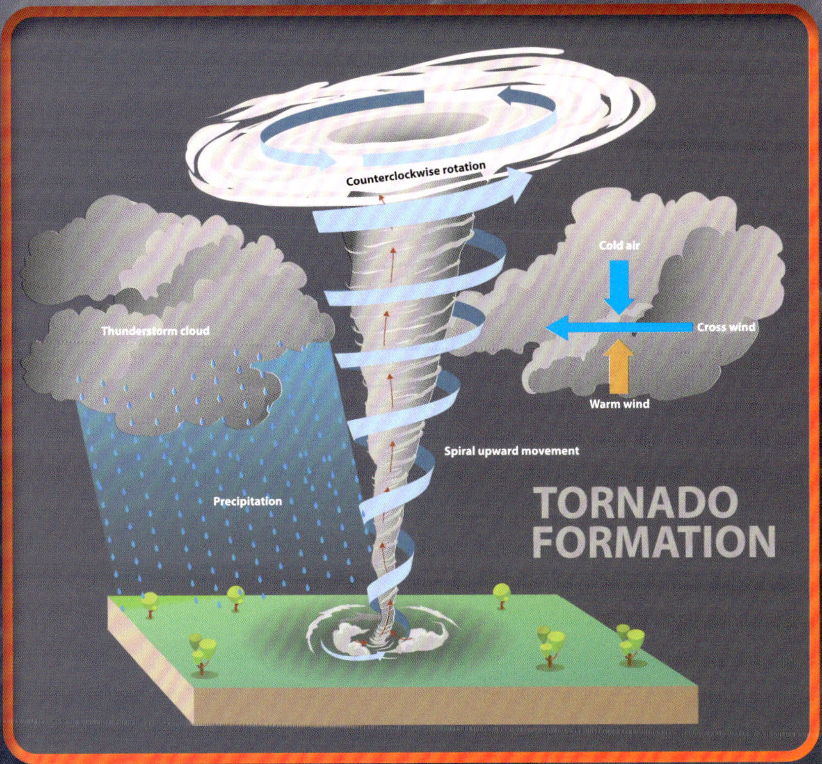

If you ever spot a cone-shaped cloud extending downward from a thunderstorm, that's a ***funnel cloud***. It could become a tornado at any second.

PICKING UP SPEED

The updraft and downdraft sometimes go up and down in a regular pattern. They begin to twist around each other and make each other stronger. This is a supercell thunderstorm. It's the most dangerous kind!

Close to the ground, the wind is slower and blows in one direction. But going higher, the wind speeds up and blows in the other direction! This is called **wind shear**.

Instability and wind shear cause a **vortex**. An example of a vortex is the spinning water that forms when you let the water drain out of your bathtub. As the water flows down the drain, it spins.

THAT'S EXTREME!

The vortex that forms out of a supercell storm is also called a funnel cloud. When the funnel cloud touches the ground, it becomes a tornado!

FASTER AND FASTER

A vortex starts to form. In a thunderstorm, the vortex is called a **mesocyclone**. Mesocyclones are usually 2 to 6 miles (3 to 10 km) wide. If a mesocyclone has formed, there's about a 50 percent chance it will turn into a tornado.

The mesocyclone gets caught in an updraft and spins faster and faster. It reaches out of the storm cloud in a swirling funnel cloud. Rain and hail pull the funnel cloud to the ground. Once it touches the ground, it becomes a tornado!

THAT'S EXTREME!

You can often hear a tornado before you can see it. A tornado's loud roar is like a freight train!

A funnel cloud often looks darker after it touches the ground, because it picks up dirt and dust.

THE TORNADO'S PATH

In the United States, tornadoes move from west to east. The tornado follows the direction of the cloud that it came from. Most tornadoes last just two to three minutes, but some last much longer.

Tornadoes are usually about 1.5 miles (2.4 km) wide. But the paths of these violent storms can be impossible to predict. The edge of a tornado could destroy all the houses on one side of a street but leave the houses on the other side completely untouched. The things picked up by a tornado's strong winds can come back down many miles (km) away.

THAT'S EXTREME!

The center of a tornado is called the "eye." Only two people have been in the eye of a tornado and lived through it. They say it's quiet, calm, and hard to breathe, with almost nonstop lightning.

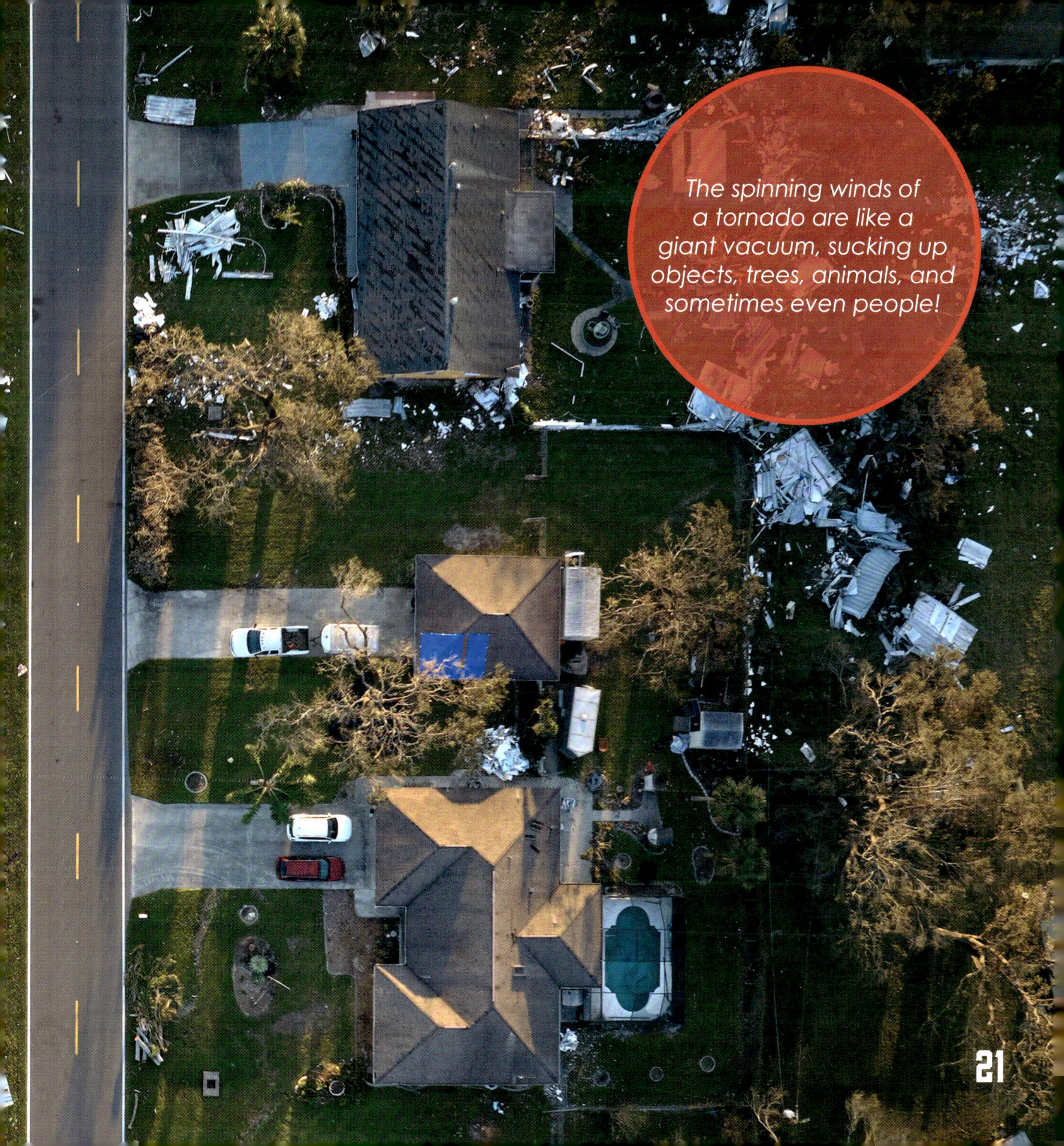

The spinning winds of a tornado are like a giant vacuum, sucking up objects, trees, animals, and sometimes even people!

THE STORM IS OVER

The heavy rain begins to let up. The strong winds slow down. The tornado is over.

Tornadoes stop when the storm becomes weaker. Changes in wind, temperature, or the storm's structure can cause the tornado to fade away.

After the storm ends, its path of destruction remains. Some houses are completely smashed. Others are fine! Trees are knocked over. Cars are damaged. **Debris** is scattered everywhere. People come out of their homes to check on each other. Firefighters and police officers arrive to help.

THAT'S EXTREME!

During a tornado, a storm cellar or the basement of your home are the safest places to be. If your home doesn't have one, stay in the most central room of your home, or even a closet. Keep away from windows!

The damage caused by a tornado can take a long time to clean up. Many times, communities come together to offer help.

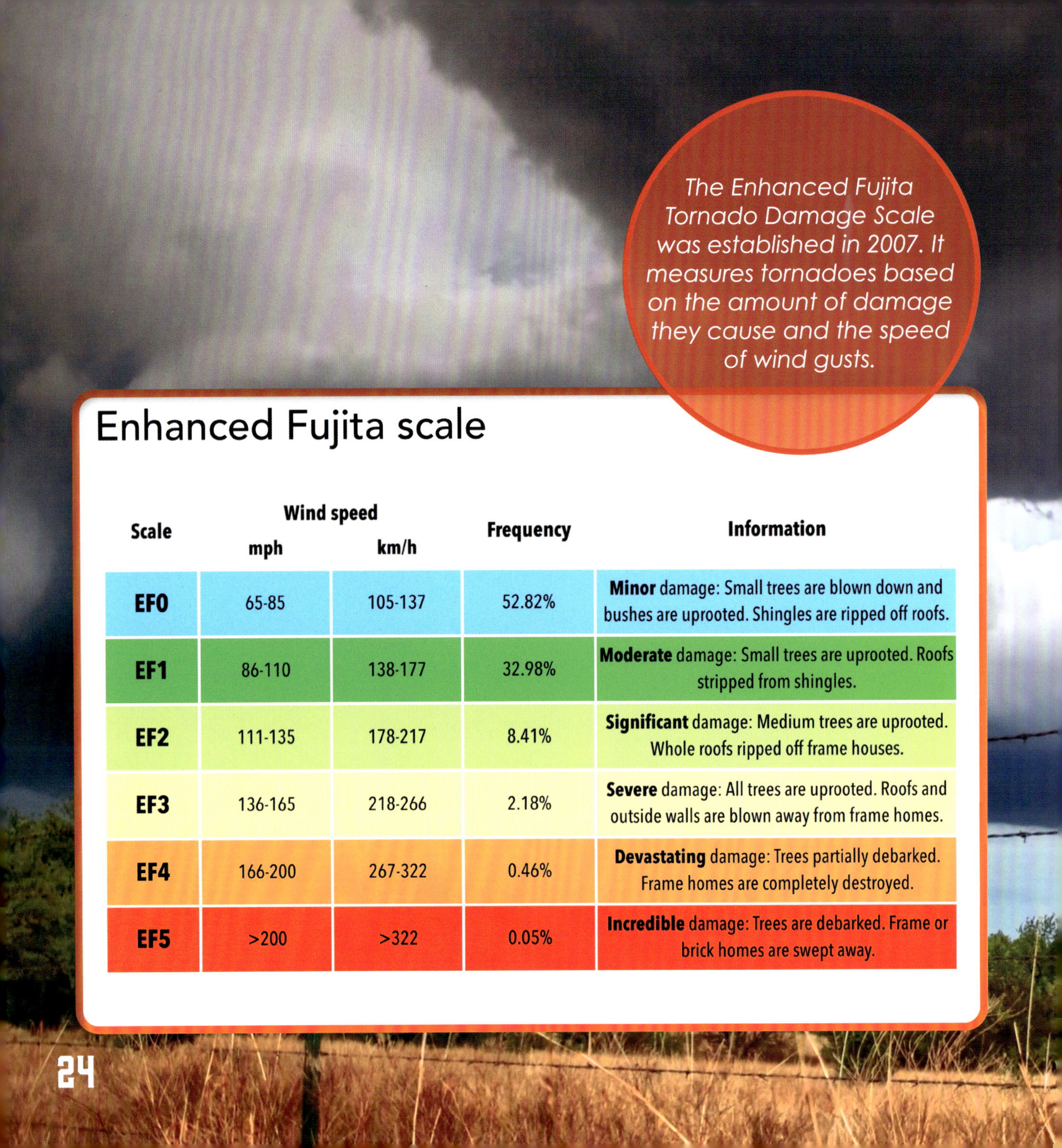

The Enhanced Fujita Tornado Damage Scale was established in 2007. It measures tornadoes based on the amount of damage they cause and the speed of wind gusts.

Enhanced Fujita scale

Scale	Wind speed mph	Wind speed km/h	Frequency	Information
EF0	65-85	105-137	52.82%	**Minor** damage: Small trees are blown down and bushes are uprooted. Shingles are ripped off roofs.
EF1	86-110	138-177	32.98%	**Moderate** damage: Small trees are uprooted. Roofs stripped from shingles.
EF2	111-135	178-217	8.41%	**Significant** damage: Medium trees are uprooted. Whole roofs ripped off frame houses.
EF3	136-165	218-266	2.18%	**Severe** damage: All trees are uprooted. Roofs and outside walls are blown away from frame homes.
EF4	166-200	267-322	0.46%	**Devastating** damage: Trees partially debarked. Frame homes are completely destroyed.
EF5	>200	>322	0.05%	**Incredible** damage: Trees are debarked. Frame or brick homes are swept away.

TORNADO FORECASTING

Weather **forecasts** try to give people enough warning so they can protect themselves. **Meteorologists** try to figure out when and where tornadoes might form. When weather conditions may result in a tornado, meteorologists announce a "tornado watch." When a tornado has been spotted, a "tornado warning" is given.

Most scientists use the Enhanced Fujita Scale to measure the strength of tornadoes. EF 0 tornadoes are the weakest and cause little harm. EF 5 tornadoes are the strongest and can blow entire houses away!

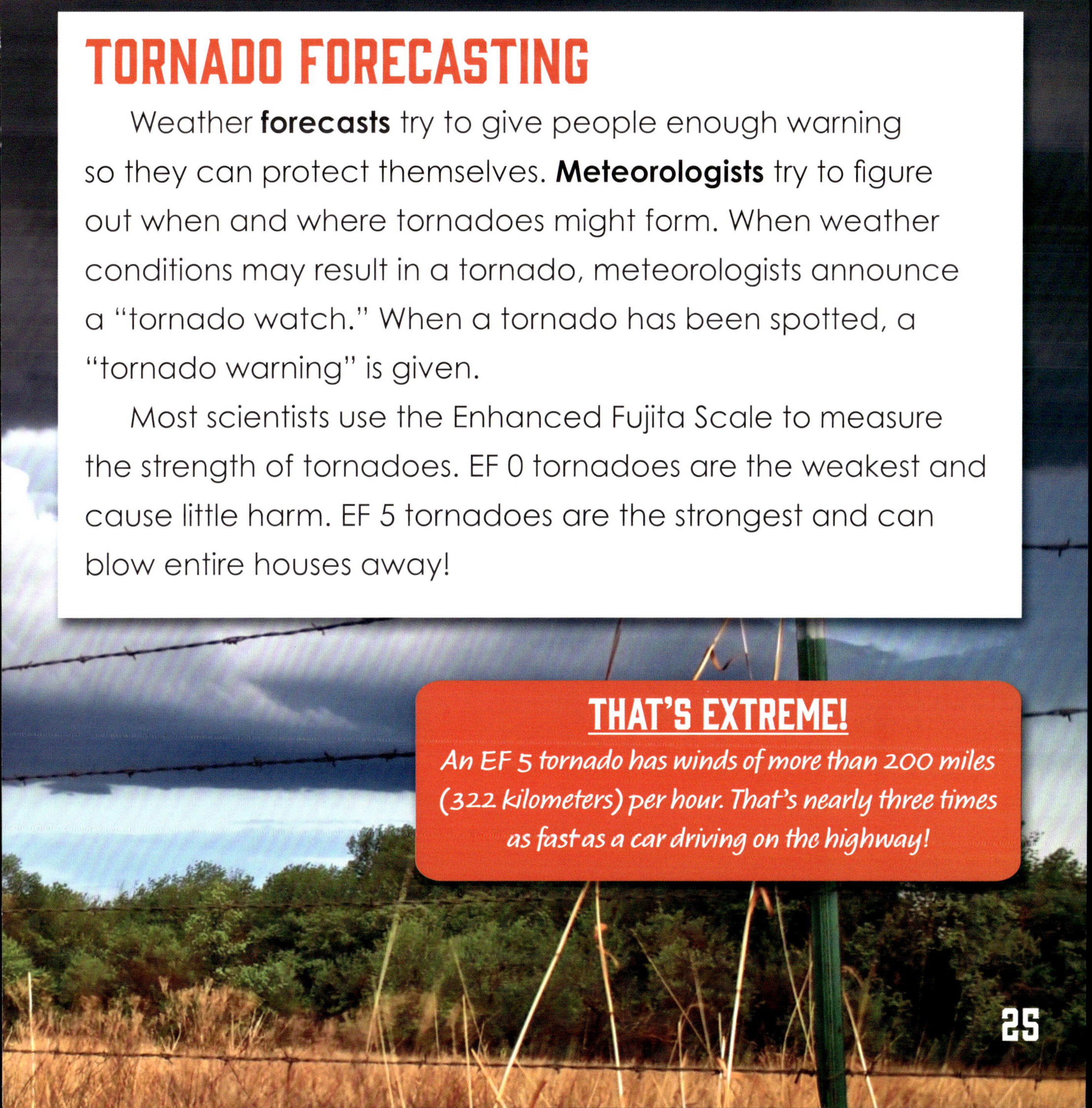

THAT'S EXTREME!

An EF 5 tornado has winds of more than 200 miles (322 kilometers) per hour. That's nearly three times as fast as a car driving on the highway!

PROTECT YOURSELF

Being prepared when a tornado hits can save lives. People in Tornado Alley often have emergency plans and safety kits ready if a tornado hits.

The first rule of tornado safety is to go to the lowest part of your house. If you don't have a basement, go to a windowless inside room such as a closet. If you're outside when a tornado hits, you should lie down in a ditch. Always protect your head. If you're in a car or a mobile home, try to find the nearest sturdy building.

If you're caught in a tornado, text for help. Don't call. Keep the phone lines open for emergency workers.

THAT'S EXTREME!

The sky might be blue when a tornado watch is given, but don't be fooled! Tornadoes can strike with little warning.

Emergency kits for a tornado should include bottled water, a first aid kit, a flashlight with extra batteries, and easy-to-eat food like crackers.

Some experts drive toward tornadoes instead of away from them! These people are called storm chasers. However, this is very dangerous and should only be done by professionals.

EXTREME WEATHER

Tornadoes are amazing—but very dangerous—natural wonders. The inside of a tornado is a fascinating and terrifying place. Luckily, it usually only lasts for a few minutes. Isn't it wild that such extreme weather can come and go so quickly, but leave behind so much destruction?

Even though very few thunderstorms turn into tornadoes, they can happen anytime and anywhere. If you see a funnel cloud, remember what you've learned. You'll know how to keep yourself safe!

THAT'S EXTREME!

Have you heard of the saying "the calm before the storm"? That's because right before a tornado hits, things can get weirdly quiet and calm.

GLOSSARY

atmosphere: the mixture of gases that surrounds a planet

debris: pieces of things that have been broken or destroyed

dense: how much mass is packed into a certain volume

downdraft: the downward movement of air

forecasts: predictions of what will happen in the future

funnel cloud: a cloud with a long shape that is wide at the top and skinny on the bottom, like an ice cream cone

humid: having a lot of moisture in the air

hurricane: a powerful storm that forms over water and causes heavy rainfall and high winds

instability: a sudden change in the weather

mesocyclone: the whirling winds inside a thunderstorm that often produce tornadoes

meteorologist: a scientist who studies the atmosphere and weather

updraft: the upward movement of air

unstable: not steady; likely to change

violent: strong and destructive

vortex: a spinning mass of water or air

wind shear: a quick change in wind speed and direction

MORE INFORMATION

BOOKS

Cappucci, Matthew. *Extreme Weather for Kids*. Beverly, MA: Quarry Books, 2024.

Locher, Wes. *Where Is Tornado Alley?* New York, NY: Penguin Random House, 2025.

Mattern, Joanne. *The Worst Tornadoes on Record*. Hallandale, FL: Mitchell Lane Publishers, 2025.

WEBSITES

Make a Tornado in a Bottle

sciencekids.co.nz/experiments/makeatornado.html

Read more about vortexes and learn how to make your own tornado!

Tornadoes

www.noaa.gov/education/resource-collections/weather-atmosphere/tornadoes

Read all about tornadoes and how to keep yourself safe.

INDEX